MW01519726

angel wings

and

other things

amanda korbelas

angel wings

and

other things

amanda korbelas

thank you
from the bottom of my heart
to all of the people
who did not give up on me
in my darkest times
you are the ones who
brought me pockets
of sunshine.

angel wings

chapter 1

m o v i n g   o n

I still love him

but in a different way

it's not my fault

my heart

couldn't make him stay.

the storm i've been chasing

he wore nothing

but confidence and fire

i fell in love with everything

that he couldn't stand about himself

that's what made him irresistible

falling in love with a storm

that wouldn't give up his

thunder.

her light burned dim

please

do not forget about her worth

because

you will eventually lose her

and

even if she stays today

her shining light

will slowly dim

a shadow so pale

her soul that was once so radiant

bright;

when her star died

so did she.

buried under the tide

the tide is pushing me farther

from shore

I can't tread your love

anymore.

the ladder of change

you are

a tide of water

ready to take me out

not to bury me

at the bottom of the ocean

but to show me that

life only happens

when you keep moving forward

by not staying in the same place

just because

I am too scared

of change.

waking up to the thought of
you, dreams really do come true

and the sun rose

with the thought

of your smile

and your warmth

wrapped around me

like the suns rays

wrap around the valley

and cradle the earth

I feel so safe in your

embrace as the moon

puts us to sleep

for yet another

night.

deep within my bones

everything that we have experienced

in our past life

and this life

those memories are locked deep

within us

and aside from whatever

somebody says

no one

can ever

take this

away from you.

a n g e l w i n g s

when I look into the mirror

I see a warrior standing right in front of me

when I look into the mirror

I see a smile that no one can shake

when I look into the mirror

I see my angel wings spread

and a heart that no one can take

I know from my stance

that I'm ready to go to war.

release your worries

I know that every morning you wake up

you take a breath and wonder how you are

going to make it through your day

I also know those butterflies you feel

can't be real

and the anxiety plays a main part

in how you act day-to-day

I know your past is still haunting your

present and future

while you destroy your mental health

as you watch it fade away

when it was you all along

that needed to control the noise

with that voice of all the okay's

and put silence to the madness in this

new yet simple way.

hush the ego

face the music

sometimes it's okay

to want to feel nothing

and

it's okay to face away from the sunshine

and stare off into the shadows

sometimes it's okay

to close the blinds for the day

and crawl under the blankets

and just listen to the melody

of the piano keys for the night

sometimes it's okay

to have alone time

to get to know yourself better

because since the beginning

it was only you in the first place.

f o o t s t e p s

walk away

when they no longer serve you

a purpose.

this is your life

this life

is your life

that you are

working so hard

to create

not theirs

so please

do not allow others

to destroy you

because they are

too lazy to create

something beautiful

on their own.

trigger

the moon is rising

and I'm underneath the sun

I can't help but complain

that you're still holding the gun

the stars across your back

match the freckles against my face

I can't help but kiss your chin

and hold your heart in case.

memories

what happened to the child in me

who ran to the park

wanting to be free

who stayed out late

to catch the summer air

nothing negative to catch

but the wind in my hair

when did we trade

this freedom for phones

trying to find love

because no one can be alone

I just want to go back to the carefree vibe

but still strive

to live the best life.

I'm ready to love you back

I made

a home out of you

when all I had to offer

was my bitterness

and hardships

that I gained

from the man before.

I'm sorry

b a y   o f   l i e s

I'm beginning

to hold my breath

longer than the last

only to watch my face turn

as blue as the water

you drowned

me in

catching you

in all of these lies

wasn't what killed me

it was the promise

you made

saying it wouldn't happen again

that did.

less of

lets have

more smiles

and less frowns

our chins facing only up

and not looking down

we need

more flowers

and less weeds

more love

and

less greed.

love is the way to everything

success story

sweetheart

look at how far you have come

remember that all success stories

do not happen over night

and that it takes time

for your roots to grip in

and embed the soil

but when you start to

regain strength

you must

and you will

push through

and be able to witness

how far you actually

came.

queen of hearts

I miss you

more than

I'd like to admit that

I can't help but fall for you

I don't know when to quit

you hold me every evening

and kiss my forehead goodbye

even hearts fall like

stars sometimes and

begin to flutter and fly.

silver lining

you are so beautiful

that even heaven itself

grounds to you

like the moon

binds itself

to the wolf.

heart of glass

when I shattered

I brought you along with me

you resembled my own emptiness

and I laughed to cause you pain

just like you made me feel that day

I didn't mean to raise my voice

and bring down your wall

to only step over the crumble and debris

I just wanted you to love me

openly and freely

just like I love(d) you

when you ignored me.

i n n e r   e n v y

I am grateful

I know I am

it's just

sometimes I get jealous

of lost time with you

you know

those hours that aren't spent with me

because you're running around your head

thinking of her.

u n c e r t a i n t y

I crave you there

but yet flinch every time you raise

your arms to only embrace my instability

you became my fire

but every time I spoke

your fire burned to coals

of uncertainty,

how I remind you

and I am willing to mourn the loss of you

the passing of our souls

never reconnecting

again

and I'm willing to give up what we could have had

because it causes too much pain to hold on

and I really hope when you find someone new

that there are little things

that she does that remind you

of me

and make you rethink what you meant to me

you should have never let go

of my hand in the first place.

chaos in the storm

after these men

came through my mind

to just ruin the place

like a storm

a damn tornado

I shut my windows and slammed

the doors - too afraid to love

and because I opened

myself up one more time

biting my lip as I sat shy

the earth brought the sunshine

to you my love

I finally see

what love should be

so thank you

for loving me.

n i g h t m a r e

sleep now child

his dreams are with someone

else.

embrace the beauty from within

poor girl

stop throwing your beauty around

like it is all you have to offer

real men want more than that

that's how you get them to stay

through intelligence

using your brain

and not being negative

in anyway.

she's so vain

in the whole world I found
someone like you

you know when someone

touches your soul

and it feels like home

a positive reward

a big fortune

that this one single soul

can bring you so much love

something sweetheart

that you're much deserving of.

i f   y o u   s t a y e d   t o   m o v e   m o u n t a i n s

and I want to move mountains

and leap across the stars

all of this sounds possible

if only it wasn't for your doubt

the only thing that doesn't validate my loneliness

is giving you up

to love

someone else.

truth or dare

I dare you

to try and love me back

just this once.

love yourself

I idolize you

not for the love you gave me

but for the love you taught

me to give to myself.

t h r o u g h   h e r   e y e s

just for a moment

just forget what it feels like

to lose control

breathe and let the fire

invade the surface of your skin

as the lightning from her eyes hissed

and created a storm of rain

that released her pain

from within.

let go of

we need to let go
of the perception that
people aren't allowed to change

you are allowed to grow
you are allowed to change
you are living for you
not for anyone else.

winter draft

you pulled me in close
with your warm summer love
only to push me away
when it got cold again.

in a flash

you keep flashing

back to my memories

where you once had a home

here is where you will find

your things packed away

with a for sale sign

i will still keep all of

your memories safe

along with your secrets and pain

just to watch you leave by tomorrow

all over again.

a n x i e t y

without his reflection

her gaze loses sight

no one can recognize intellect

when the heart does not

feel right.

but then again

when my name lingers off of your lips

it leaves me wanting more

but then again

so does whiskey

at the bottom of every glass.

h e a r t   a n d   t h e   m i n d

my mind and heart

think and feel two different ways

one's filled with thoughts and the other

is in a daze

it thinks out the logic

about you and I

but my heart says to make no sudden changes

because she's not ready to say goodbye

others could come and go

but none of them have caught my eye

the day you walked into my life

you set the bar so high

so I guess there's no thinking anything through

because you're the one who has my heart

I am so in love with you.

burned

you are so beautiful

I whispered

just like a burning flame

but every time I get too close

I get burned

somehow

you have me in this trance

which makes me always run back

to add more wood to your flame

before you burn out

instead of me.

as she whispered

as I screamed with rage

telling you to leave

you finally left

even though my heart whispered

please stay.

e m p t y

a stranded cabin
in the middle of winter
probably gets pretty lonely

as it grows old
and gets consumed with cob webs
and empty steps

the funny irony here is
I am at home
somewhere warm
with somebody who claims to love me

as my thoughts wonder to the back of my mind
to a place where I feel safe
I still can't help but feel
empty.

c l o s e d   h a n d s

why is it that every time I give you my love

you never open your hands in gratitude

and when I show the arch of my spine

and curl in my shoulders ready to retreat

you're finally ready to give me your(s)

hands.

and

chapter 2

A n d

yet I bare my naked body to you

you are like snake skin

that I keep shedding

and you grow back on me

thicker and stronger

you carry my weight

when life gets tough

when we hit a new chapter

you - we

shed again

we grow

we grip

you constrict

I can't breathe

but won't have it any other way.

A n d

when you lay

wrapped up and puzzled to my body

I remember I don't want to solve this problem

I just want to lay

wrapped up

and puzzled with you.

A n d

I can't see

what is right there

in front of me

without your presence

as the fog thickens

I can't help but feel

lost without you

signal and sway

your arms toward the

ocean view and let the

lighthouse help me

find you.

A n d

thank you

for holding my reputation

to the sky

showing every one

I am better than something

I once tried

for you believing in me

made everyone start to see

a different love and positive light

in me.

A n d

I'm going to write you a letter

and mail it away

you will probably always remain

curious of what it had to say

I loved you so much

but today is the day

that I take our memories together

and tuck them away.

A n d

we're stronger than ever

you and I move with the storm

you can be on the same track as us

or you can be torn

apart by our

t o r n a d o .

And

do not cry

sweet dove

as your days are not over

your wings will heal

and you will be able to soar

above mountains

until then

rest

because your day is almost

h e r e .

A n d

at last

my love

I have you in my life

it only took forever

to get you to this point

I hope you are no longer

hurting and let go of

your sorrow to

since mine has left and passed

all i need to ask you-

do you believe in angels

because God has given me to you

he knew you would protect me

in everything that we do.

.

And

if you give me your love

I will give you my light

baby just choose

will it be

fight or flight.

A n d

under these scars

was once a girl

who would do anything

for love.

A n d

love is not cruel

love is wise

when your love burns down to coals

you do not leave it

nor abandon

you must grab another log to re-light it

ignite it

so it can make it

until morning

finally

i feel his hot body

burrowed into mine

and I just realized I rekindled a flame

that deserved to stay warm.

A n d

I can't help but think

that without you my back would wilt

and I'd lose my colour

you see

you're the one who makes me

so please bring me your

sunshine.

A n d

when I hit rock bottom

you were right there

you were like an angel on my shoulder

you showed me you cared

It's a love no one ever hears about

a love that's hard to find

a love that I need most

in my life.

A n d

how you love yourself

gives others the strength

and opportunity

to love you back.

A n d

you have me high on something

and it's not just your love

there is some place where this is coming from

maybe from up above?

o u r   o w n   h e a v e n

And

how can a creature

be so beautiful

yet deadly

just like my love for you.

A n d

when you touch someones soul

the way they yearn to be touched

who says you can't water somebody else's garden?

and watch them blossom first.

A n d

my mind started

as an empty garden

but you made me

bloom

blossom

into something beautiful.

A n d

there is so much distance

between us

from room to room

but yet I am writing lullabies

in thought of you.

A n d

you cursed me

and have me locked under your spell

they say never make love to an angel

that once fell.

A n d

yet I cry rivers for you

but

the happy tears

you bring me to my knees

and I couldn't be more comfortable

grounding myself

to the earth

and giving my heart and soul

to you.

A n d

you were something beautiful

even with your cracked

and weathered skin.

A n d

she doesn't have to

take her clothes off

to be intimate with you

you just have to listen

to the love

that is playing off

of her heart.

A n d

tell me when it's safe to love you again

in the mix I don't get hurt again

because loving you the first time

hurt too much.

other things

chapter 3

signed, your biggest fan

I applaud you

your appearance drawn out like a flower

I stand by you

even if you do not see me there

I am your biggest fan

up close or faraway

even if it doesn't look like I care.

i c r a v e f o r e v e r

I want to be the women

who lives in your memories

and the one who

still makes it into

your future.

across my body

speak to me

in a language that I can only

understand

follow your tongue across my body

instead of your hand

disguise your love for me

and let it be known

love me

with an honest

tongue.

good morning my love

good morning my love

thank you for the beautiful message

that got me up this morning

for keeping me going

allowing me to shed my tears and the mask

that I take off and put back on

when the sun comes up

thank you for the truth you speak so nobly

without saying a word

the power you hold

when you touch my skin and all you do is smile

good morning my love

thank you for keeping me going just a bit longer

in this race we call life.

I have infinite words

I could write infinite words

to form a sentence

to create a paragraph

on how much you mean to me

I could write in cursive

and stamp my heart and send it to you freely

you're my metaphor that's added

to my simile

I love you to the stars and back

you're my hyperbole

so thank you for being my soul mate

you make my poetry.

sweet dreams

you my love

were destined to be my song bird

as you shower me with love

in the morning

and kiss my forehead softly

before bed

as you speak kind words

to me daily

as I lay my head

down for bed.

the northern star

white fragment sheds off of the Northern star

even something so beautiful

can fall.

the blue monarch

it is the blue in your eyes

that calms those very

butterflies

you made me feel

earlier.

one man symphony

just love me in the crossfire

hold me a bit tighter

whisper sweet thoughts

and laugh with me a bit longer

let me tell you

how much you mean to me

be my one man symphony.

summer storm

you felt like rain

on a summer day

like eating ice cream

in the pouring rain

you were different

they were the same

but I'd still choose you

over and over again.

her legacy

they wonder

why she writes

so vividly

and in code

it's so her younger self

can realize

that she has come so far.

my garden

I lust

for the very flowers

that helped us

bloom.

empty canvas

the way we went together

was like white

and coloured paints-

as you brightened my darkest moments

I filled your canvas with dreams

that every time we looked

at one another

we could not help but sketch out

different lives that we wanted to live

until it was our type of masterpiece.

fuel

I just want to kiss your neck

touch your soul

let you in

and lose control

let me feel your fire.

changes

you

the stars

a twinkling blue

a secret so destined

between me and you

the third season is here

yet she won't stay

the orange tattered leaves die

on this cold

winter day.

sunshine

I hope that everyone

finds their own sunshine

in today's rain

and everyone finds

a little happiness

in the little things.

security blanket

I want you

to hold me

like my puppy

blanket once did

through the tears and the laughter

the rips and the chatter

of growing up

and missing who I used to be.

the great wall

her walls

are still too high

she needs kind words

to break them down.

bare skin

I constantly touch you

in hope that you would notice

that I need to receive your love back

and

I constantly look at you

in hope that you would notice

that I didn't need make-up

or this expensive dress

and

you would love me

for me

in just my bare skin.

imperfection is perfection

first time

and

he just opened me up just like that

like he has already read this novel

like he has already touched this exact spot more

than once

he just ripped me open

so clean

yet so raw

he knew me

yet this was our first time

meeting.

twin flame

through the good and the bad

be my beacon of light

guide me through the good

and the bad

when I am happy

or when I am mad

just please

don't give up on me.

like he once did

w h o ?

now

who could get tired

of kissing someone like you?

you open me up into a world of beauty

to only imagine the clarity to love someone

like me back.

f r i c t i o n

when our souls collide

it isn't just a storm holding us

together.

eleven to midnight

11:49pm

and I feel my mouth open

and my lower lip scratch up

against your soft facial hair

I begin to grip you so tight

after everything you had put me through

with all of the anger I felt that night

and in that moment

I realize you're not the enemy

I am . . was

so I start to release my grip

just like a boa constrictor

and cuddle you

the way you were meant for me.

you make me

hot madness

the eager craving of your lips sticking to mine

like honey on a hot summer day

the clasp of my bra

which releases the tension

as your hands run down the arch of my back

your eyes

where I lose all grounds of reality

where love awakens your light

and I realize

I am right where I need to be.

h e r

her inner essence

sparked something wild in his heart

and the stars and the moon

could not keep those two apart.

I can't imagine

can you imagine

an ocean without waves?

a sky without clouds?

lungs without a breath?

precisely

it's just like me

without you.

s o u l   m a t e

that exact moment

when our eyes locked

my stomach had already captured

and gathered up all of

the butterflies

and placed them into

a jar

and that was the moment

my soul

knew you were

the one.

r e a d y   o r   n o t ,   h e r e   I   c o m e

you

there is something so beautiful

in the fact that you

came looking for me

when I hid from the world

it was just like

our very own game

of hide and seek.

right under your nose

you looked

right into me

like I have been studied

so easily

and this is what

you mean to me

something so beautiful

and freeing.

and this whole time
she was a warrior
just her weapon of choice
was a pen.

the end.

thank you

for all that you do

you helped create the whirl wind

between me and you

of raw emotion

x x

a k